Beginner's Guide to Online Side Hustles

60+ simple ways to earn online fast and build repeatable passive income streams

Table of Contents

Introduction

Our world's changing. It's not new news that society is shifting toward a more entrepreneurial economy. In an environment of job and social security benefits uncertainty, it's essential you take control of your future.

This means finding ways to make money independently. For you that could mean helping ends meet. It could also mean pursuing financial freedom. Your goal could be to grow a new venture. Alternatively, it could be to simply develop a profitable sideline.

Whatever it means to you, there are more opportunities than ever. It's time to buy into the idea of "multiple streams of income."

This is not a new concept. The principles have been doing the round for decades. Rich Dad, Poor Dad was driving the narrative decades ago.

And it's not dirty to want to make a bit more cash. Your challenge is to monetize your ideas successfully.

This book isn't the holy grail. It's there to give you a basic framework for what's out there. It's got simple aspirations – to expose those new to the side hustle concept to a range of opportunities.

What should you be doing to make money?

The easiest way would be to work with what you've already got and know. Start by trying to monetize your expertise. But keep in mind, you must have something to offer that's in demand.

We all have great ideas but that doesn't mean that will make you money. As a starting point, ask people what they want – then build it. "Building it" could mean, for example, giving guidance to someone looking for help on how to write a proposal.

You could service that need in many ways, simply sitting from your sofa. You could coach them via Skype. You could write an eBook on the topic and sell it on Amazon. You could create a course that you sell on your website or specific platforms designed to sell courses. You could create an online webinar. You could build a YouTube channel…

The key to all of these is that you can do them all from the comfort of your own home. That's really what this is about.

How do you find clients? Go to where they are looking for a specific service – then provide the service. That's essentially what this is about. It really comes down to how you go about doing it. These are areas we cover in the book.

You might not see yourself as an entrepreneur, but you need to cultivate an entrepreneurial mindset. And in order to do that you need to create systems to develop a proven process that makes it easier for you.

You want to make sure you are being efficient and effective. For example, you don't want to be creating everything from scratch each time. That defeats the object of giving you some form of freedom. This is something we'll touch on as well.

Framing your Approach

How do I start? Just start anywhere.

This is about making the most of available technology and cheap resources to generate income.

You can sit around thinking about the perfect idea or how to create the perfect service. But before you know it a couple of months. Maybe even years.

In the meantime, the world's moved on and you're still stuck in the concept phase. It's like storing away your favorite shirt, only to pull it out one day and realize big collars went out of fashion a long time ago.

You don't need to have all the answers but start with the end in mind – base it on your values; who you are and who you're not. That way you can get more clarity on what you're willing to do. But this is also where having systems in place make sense. You can't just shoot from the hip and hope to achieve a stable and sustainable income stream.

Your system may not be perfect but keep in mind whether what you are doing is repeatable and scalable.

Crafting something from scratch each time may satisfy your artistic urges. But it's a lot more difficult to turn it into an income stream with growth potential. The goal is to create structures for freedom, engineering an architecture to remove stress from the process. That includes having the right people around you.

It's trial and error so it may take time. But it's important.

But that's further down the line and really beyond the scope of this book. It's about keeping things uncomplicated. So, a great place to start is by doing simple gigs.

Online Income Opportunities

There are so many sites online that offer work-at-home opportunities. Some are more legitimate than others.

Many are very established, while you'll be sure to find your fill of fly–by-night sites. One rule of thumb is to never pay to sign up for any of them. That screams scam. Or multi-level marketing. Or both.

This book isn't about taking issue with MLM. It's just that for those starting out there are far easier ways to make a few dollars. But if you see your future millions in MLM, then go for it.

Many online opportunities (including in this book) have referral schemes. For example, for Postloop, Clickworker and Prolific Academic you may earn a commission for directing others to their site if they sign up. You get paid by the company, not the person signing up.

Even in relation to the ideas in this book, I would also always suggest doing your own due diligence on top, googling the name of the site plus the word "review" or "scam" to see what comes up. That way you're learning from the experiences of the many.

Freelance Marketplaces

Fundamentally, one of the easiest ways to make money online is to find "marketplaces". The internet is one big marketplace, anyway, with over two billion shoppers. Use it! Whether it's Google or Facebook, YouTube or Twitter, it's there to be used. You will never be short of potential customers.

As a side hustler, it's almost a rite of passage to dip your toe into specific freelance marketplaces.

These sites are designed to allow you to sell your skills to the highest / lowest bidders, whether that involves you as a content writer, coder, logo designer, voiceover professional or even someone that can put together a jingle.

People can earn a serious amount of cash on these sites. Just don't join the race to the bottom and heavily discount your hard-earned skills.

Here are some to consider:

Upwork: Upwork hires and manages freelancers online. It's well established and one of the biggest platforms out there, having swallowed up a few competitors in recent years. https://www.upwork.com

Fiverr: A popular marketplace. It used to be simply about earning five dollars per gig (hence the name) but now you can customize each one and earn a whole lot more.

Even if you do end up charging five dollars, you've got to think about building up a portfolio of your work. That way you're going to be able to prove to potential clients that you've got what it takes to do a job before graduating to charge more. https://www.fiverr.com

PeoplePerHour: It's a marketplace for freelance talent like Fiverr and Upwork, only it's more selective on those with a service to sell and is based out of the UK. As a result, you'll likely see a better-quality mix – at least, that's been my experience.

It's also got one of the best referral programs out there. You can earn $45 each time you invite a friend and they start their first project there (via invitation email and not via referral links). https://www.peopleperhour.com/dashboard

Gigbucks: Another marketplace site, so offering similar dynamics to Fiverr etc.http://gigbucks.com

Fivesquid: Think Fiverr, only based out of the UK and denominated in pound sterling. https://www.fivesquid.com

Micro Jobs

You don't have to have a doctorate to make money through side hustles online. You just have to be willing to put the effort in.

There are plenty of micro jobs out there that you can use to start with. These tend to be at the lower skill end of the equation, which in turn means lower pay. But if you have time and patience you can pick up quite a few dollars reasonably easily.

ClixSense: One of the more popular pay-per-click sites, which allows you to make money taking surveys, viewing ads and its affiliate program. www.clixsense.com

MTurk: This is a very popular one with a lot of people, offering a variety of micro jobs. It's under the banner of Amazon so I'd like to think it's reliable. It's US-centric so not one that everyone can use. https://www.mturk.com/mturk/welcome

Clickworker: This is one of the simpler sites to make a few dollars doing micro tasks, clicking to register responses.Many of these tasks require little or no form of expertise and can vary from providing a "like" on Facebook pages, checking search engine results for a topic to gauging the quality of a voice recording. There are plenty of tasks if you manage to pass the easy tests. https://www.clickworker.com

OneSpace: Having taken over CrowdSource, OneSpace has a more expanded platform. This is another micro task site, that allows for copywriting, data, moderation and transcription roles. Pass a few tests and you'll get access to plenty of tasks offering a least a few dollars a time. https://work.onespace.com

Transcription

Transcription isn't to everyone's tastes but there always seems to be work here, listening in on audios and transcribing the information. It's at the lower skills end but you can make money.

TranscribeMe: Take the test first to see whether you're accepted. Work as much as you like or as little (in other words until you are thoroughly bored is my guess). https://workhub.transcribeme.com/Account/Register.

Rev: This is similar to above. I've seen it written that Rev's pay works out to about $24 to $39 per audio hour but don't be misled into thinking that represents a straight hour of work. https://www.rev.com/freelancers/transcription

Tigerfish: One of the most established in this space (apparently, it's been around since 1989). You'll have to pass the test as with the others. The company doesn't share information on pay rates, method, and job frequency until you apply. http://tigerfish.com/employment

Affiliate Marketing

Once you've got to grips with the basics online, you can graduate to other ways to make money. For example, if you are thinking of selling something online, you don't actually have to even create your own product to make money.

You can simply help someone that already has done so. All you have to do is send internet traffic through a link to that product, wherever it is online, and everything after that is out of your hands.

How does it work? Affiliate marketing is a way of making money online whereby you "as a publisher" earn a commission for helping another business promote their products, services or business opportunity.

To do so, you first have to sign up as an affiliate to promote a company's products or services. Next, you find ways to promote the products. This can be by emailing your distribution list. Alternatively, you could publish ads, web pages, blog posts, and videos to promote the products. This can be through Facebook, Twitter or other social media platforms.

You then earn a commission if and when you make a sale for the company. That's the crux of it. You're not creating the product –

you're simply helping to sell it and getting paid for any success you have.

You can use this strategy in association with other income strategies, or you can focus entirely on earning money this way.

Affiliate marketing can become a huge part of a passive income strategy. But it's important to do it with integrity. People often react negatively about it because some "influencers" recommend products and services primarily for the commissions, and not because they help. So be responsible in what you are promoting.

Where to start?

Amazon Affiliates: There are so many affiliate platforms you can use. The most obvious and easiest to start with is Amazon Affiliates. It may not pay the best commission, but it does have brand integrity and people are always willing to trust what they buy on Amazon.

This all sounds good but it's not easy. To make decent money, you must think beyond just low-end items and target big ticket products.

ClickBank: Aside from the program of Amazon (https://affiliate-program.amazon.com), ClickBank probably has the most well-known affiliate program out there, where you can make money effectively marketing someone else's products. Plus, while they don't have an affiliate program for referring new affiliates you can earn extra commission by referring additional product vendors to ClickBank. www.clickbank.com

If you have a finance industry bias, you can try a range of finance affiliates:

Motif Investing: Motif Investing is a company that offers their own alternative to packaged investment portfolios like mutual funds, ETFs or the combined service of robo-advisors. Earn commissions for each customer referred to Motif from your website. https://www.motif.com

RealtyShares: Earn passive income by directly investing in properties from around the US. www.realtyshares.com

Betterment: Betterment is an online investment company based in New York City. In terms of referrals, for every friend who signs up and funds the account, you get 30 days free, and each friend gets 3 months free. As a bonus, when your first 3 friends fund, you get an extra free year. https://www.betterment.com

Wealthfront: Wealthfront is an all-in-one solution that helps you build a free financial plan for the life you want and automate your investments at a low cost. The Wealthfront Invite Program allows you to lower your annual advisory fee. Invite your friends and they'll waive fees on an additional $5,000 for both you and your friend when they fund an account.

Working via your Phone

YouGov: I'm not a major fan of surveys usually, as not everyone can get access to them and it can take ages to monetize. But YouGov is easy to do, has surveys available all around the world and you can do it on the go on your phone. https://yougov.co.uk

MindSwarms. Get paid to share your opinions: mobile video surveys. Some surveys pay $50-$75, though it's quite difficult to get onto most of them, particularly if you are outside of the US. https://www.mindswarms.com

MobileExpressions: This one can only be downloaded on iPhones. After you've installed it for one week, you get to play an instant rewards game for a prize. Not all regions are eligible for this one. https://www.mobilexpression.com

Writing

Writing opportunities come in a variety of shades. Blogging is one angle. This is beyond the scope of a basic approach to online income and there are plenty of resources out there on this. And it's not an overnight income earner so is different from a lot of ideas here.

It can certainly be a passive income, but it takes a lot of hard work. A lot more effort and planning than a lot of people realize. You've got to appreciate that every time you write a post, it could be a vehicle for income. The more you write, the better. Or rather, the more quality you write, the better.

It's also a low-cost income generator, as you can set up a blog for free. So find your topic, hopefully one you're passionate about, check there's a market for it, have great content and add value.

Anyway, enough on blogging. There are plenty of sites that allow you to earn using your writing skills. Some are looking for skilled, experienced writers. Others are happy to accept those that are less established. Below is a mix of both. And you can expect the pay to reflect your level of skill as well.

iWriter: For those starting out in the writing space, this could be a starting point. The problem is that it doesn't pay that well (as low as $1 for a 300 to 500-word article). But this can be used for building up your skills and portfolio before trying your luck elsewhere. http://www.iwriter.com

Freelancer: Freelancer isn't just for writing but there are plenty of opportunities here. Hundreds of freelance jobs across a variety of areas. For some tasks, the pricing can be poor and uncompetitive, so that can be an issue in terms of being able to get work, but there are always jobs there to bid for. https://www.freelancer.com

ListVerse: Write a Top 10 Lists on everything under the sun. They are very selective as to what lists they accept (i.e. I've tried and failed in getting a list accepted) but if they do publish your piece, they pay $100 for a list. http://listverse.com

International Living: If you like to travel and have a story to tell, this online magazine might be the site for you. A lot of the articles are from expats living away from their home country. The pay's pretty good as well if they accept your articles. http://internationalliving.com

Postloop: You get paid to write in forums and on blogs. It's not the most trying intellectually and there's always 'work' to be had if you sign up for enough forums / blogs. It's not going to pay big money, though people have been known to earn $5-$10 a day on it. https://www.postloop.com

The Forum Wheel: Similar forum writing dynamic to Postloop, only newer and less established. If you can't get onto Postloop (you need to pass a writing test first), check out this one as they have a lower entry barrier. http://theforumwheel.com

WritersDomain: The site strives "to produce high-quality, original content for our clients". https://www.writersdomain.net

Babble: This is Disney's parenting website. They want to get stories that discuss parenting from an unusual angle or offer fresh advice on a parenting topic. http://www.babble.com

Motley Fool: This is a very respected site and it's quite competitive. If you like writing about personal finance and investing, this may be the site for you. It's a great way to build up a portfolio. They pay around $50-$100 for pieces. http://www.fool.com

MakeaLivingWriting.com. Another writing blog. Topics include blogging, time management, and how to find writing jobs. http://www.makealivingwriting.com/why-i-pay-writers/

Selling your Stuff

Ebay.com is a well-established place for selling stuff you don't want anymore. But don't forget Craigslist.com and Facebook groups for reselling. If you have specialist items to sell, whether they're your own creations or things you want to get rid of, it's worth thinking about these sites as well:

Etsy.com: This is the largest peer-to-peer marketplace for handcrafted items. You can offload everything in your own storefront from creations for the home and office to weddings and birthdays.

Storenvy: This is another site for selling your own unique clothing designs, as well as arts and crafts.

iCraft: It's similar to the other sites, this is for selling handmade items. www.iCraftGifts.com

Poshmark: If you have designer clothes to get rid of, try the Poshmark.com app. You can take a photo and list an item within minutes.

Swap.com: If you want to offload female and children's clothes, you can go through Swap's online consignment store to earn cash.

Zazzle: Zazzle offers you three ways to make money online: design your own products, make your own products and promote Zazzle products. http://www.zazzle.com

Bookscouter: Over the years you would have built up a collection of books. Why don't you sell your used ones onlinefor extra money? http://bookscouter.com

Teaching and Coaching

The internet is the education system of the future. Use your current skills to earn.

Italki: Offer your services teaching a foreign language. Note: they are not currently looking for individuals looking to teach English so unless you have another language to work with it might not be for you. https://www.italki.com

InstaEdu (also known as Chegg Tutors): Provide online tutoring and homework help on demand. You apply and they decide whether the skill you have to offer is relevant to their client base. https://instaedu.com

TutsPlus.com. EnvatoTuts+ is a tutorial site with thousands of videos, articles, and tutorials to help people learn new skills. The tutorials range from crafting projects to learning how to code a website. It pays around $50 for articles. http://tutsplus.com/teach

Coach.me: If you have coaching skills there are several platforms can use to pitch your services. This is a popular site for using your skills. https://www.coach.me

Testing

A number of sites out there test websites and mobile apps. For some you simply need to be able to speak into your laptop microphone and get recorded reviewing a site. These types of sites tend to pay at least $10 per review but they are getting more popular so there may not always be jobs.

UserTesting: Website and mobile app reviewing. It's quite popular now so you may not get as many gigs on it as you could in the past, but it could be a good earner if you get regularly selected. http://www.usertesting.com

What Users Do: Another online testing site with testers reviewing sites etc. Less well known than UserTesting so may offer up more jobs for you. https://www.whatusersdo.com

UserLytics: Same pattern as above, though less established. www.userlytics.com

ErliBird: Recruits and runs targeted real-world focus groups for beta testing, user experience testing, or market research. Get paid for giving feedback.

http://www.erlibird.com

Beta Family: A crowdtesting platform for beta testing iOS and Android applications so a mobile approach to testing. https://betafamily.com

UTest: If you're any good with code this might be for you. And it pays well. Unfortunately, not all of us are so are missing out on the better rates here as a software tester. http://www.utest.com

UsabilityHub: Another reviewing site. Doesn't monetize as quickly as UserTesting or What Users Do but worth having in your portfolio. https://usabilityhub.com

Testbirds: Tests websites and apps. Pays better than UsabilityHub but the testing processes can take a fair bit longer.http://www.testbirds.com

Online Surveys

Surveys don't work for everyone, and I tend to avoid them as they take too long to monetize. But below are a few to consider.

Prolific Academic: Easily my most favored survey site. The surveys are academic in nature (hence the name) put together by university faculties. As a result, they are a lot more interesting that most of the consumer surveys and also pays more than them as well, paying between $1 to $5 for a short survey. Denominated in pound sterling. https://prolific.ac/rp?ref=NSHB7ZGW

Paid Surveys at Home: Another option for surveys. Haven't tried but have seen it recommended. http://www.paid-surveys-at-home.com

Swagbucks: Sign up for Swagbucks which rewards you for surveys as well as simply surfing the web, watching videos and playing games. www.swagbucks.com

"Different"

There are so many easy money-making opportunities out there. In a matter of hours, you could be making a few dollars here or there. Look at it as trial and error – not all will suit you.

Humanatic: If you like to listen in on customer services calls then this one's for you. Maybe not for everyone as it can get tedious, but if you manage your time you may do ok. www.humanatic.com

SliceThePie: It's a site that was created to give aspiring musicians a chance to have their music rated and reviewed. It's popular and users will swear by it. Unfortunately, it's not available to all geographic regions. www.slicethepie.com

Foap: With a smartphone we're all amateur photographers. Why not try to make money that way? There's an app called Foap that allows you to turn your smartphone photos into cash. You upload photo to Foap's marketplace. Someone buys the license to your photo for $10. You make $5. https://www.foap.com

SBK Center: It's "a market research study of direct mail and email marketing materials received by consumers. In exchange for sending us your mail and email solicitations, we will compensate you for those items you might otherwise throw away". In return you get gift cards / Visa prepaid cards as compensation. http://www.sbkcenter.com/consumer.html

Blue Mountain Arts: Ever thought of writing for a greeting card company? If you see yourself as a poet, you can earn $300 for every poem this company publishes. Why not give it a go? http://www.sps.com/help/writers_guidelines.html

Task Rabbit: If you don't mind doing chores for other people you can always try Task Rabbit. Admittedly, you may have to leave the comfort of your own home. That could be mowing the lawn or walking a dog. It's an easy way to make a few dollars. https://www.taskrabbit.com

Courses

There are several reasons why creating your own online digital products make sense, whether we're talking about eBooks on Amazon or online courses on the platforms suggested.

Firstly, products. It may be a pipedream, but you can also live anywhere if you create and sell them online. Because they are often high margin products, it is possible to make good money.

It's not easy, particularly as everyone else is trying to get in a gig. It's easy to dream about making money while you are laying on a beach or while you sleep.

But if you get it right you can actually do that. It is a lot of work. Also great is that you build it once and make money forever, particularly if you become an expert in your field. Finally, if you do operate solely in the digital online space, you can forget about delivery issues – at least in the conventional sense. Once you have your systems in place you can set and forget.

Here a few useful sites:

Udemy: Udemy is one of the most popular platforms for creating a course around any skill — or element of a skill — you can teach. When it works well, it's a great passive income option. But it will take some time investment to get it going. https://www.udemy.com

Teachable: This is one of the easiest and most affordable platforms to use for creating, hosting and selling your online courses. They also have a ton of free educational resources about how to get started with creating an online course. https://teachable.com

Customer Service Jobs

Unlike most of the links above, these could be considered more like "proper job" opportunities working for a company in comparison to some of the freelance work-at-home opportunities. Although some of the role may be phone based, they do require online access. Unfortunately for many, these roles are largely restricted to North America.

West at Home: Another customer service job for North American workers only. They apparently employ thousands of home-based agents located across the country. http://apply.aloricaathome.com/index.html

TeleTech: Alongside its call center workers, TeleTech also hires home workers. Pay is said to range from $8.50 to $10.50 per hour, in addition to some benefits. https://www.ttecjobs.com/en

VIPdesk Connect: This is another 24/7 customer service company that outsources its requirements to those that want to work for them. Pay is said to be from $9.16 to $15.33 per hour, plus benefits. http://vipdeskconnect.com/current-openings/

Structuring your Side Hustle

You could do gigs here and there, and that's fine if that works for you. Alternatively, you can turn these opportunities into a sustainable income stream.

This book is mainly about internet-related opportunities. But you can try out all manner of opportunities online or offline: teaching a foreign language, babysitting, creating websites, cleaning houses, repairing cars, delivering meals…The list can go on and on.

But how can you go about framing your side hustles into something that delivers for you? Here's a simple approach:

1. Pick target goal – e.g. you want to build steady income (say, $100 per week) through writing.
2. Choose a channel to put it through – e.g. you want to create a blog, freelance for websites or write a book.
3. Bootstrap it initially – once you've gained traction you can outsource the low-value work. But when you're first finding your feet, hold onto your cash and roll up your sleeves. And you don't even have to reinvent things. There are plenty of resources already out there that work. That's what the internet is for.
4. Embrace technology – for efficiency, technology is your friend.
5. Share – if you're not one for social media, I suggest you adopt it quickly. Whether you choose to make your money online or offline, sharing your message / vision / product / service and so on is an important step.
6. Collaborate – you can go a lot further with the help of others than you can by yourself. This could mean sharing ideas on a forum, using someone else's mailing list or running a project alongside another party.
7. Bottle it – if you see traction, jump on it and run with it. You could be onto something good and you simply don't know how long it will last. And if it doesn't

work? Change your approach and test it out. Or dump it if you've given it a good go. Then go back to point 1).

Be prepared to start small. Try out a few gigs here and there first of all. You may have huge aspirations, but you've got to learn how to walk before you can run.

How much should be charging? It's really going to depend on your goals. If your goal is to stop working for others but to work for yourself, you've got to think about how to make your side hustle worth your time and energy.

To fully take control of opportunities you may have to shift your mindset. The first change is moving from a per-hour work mentality to one based on contracts and projects. The next transition is to change from being a provider of services to a producer of products.

Think about it. You could start out freelance writing for $5 to $50 an article, shift into offering $500 to $2,000 monthly packages to legitimate businesses. From there, you can repackage what you have to offer into a "how to" guide for sale. That could, for example, be in eBook or online course.

You don't have to write War and Peace. Simply target something from 5,000 to 20,000 words. That's the sweet spot. Here, you leverage pre-existing market place – e.g. iTunes and Amazon – and set out to solve a problem for beginners. A bit like this book really. Find the right keywords, price it rightly (i.e. don't go crazy on price) and you'll be on the right track.

The important thing is to grow something beyond a job. You've got to start thinking as a business owner.

The 'FIRE' (Financial Independence, Retire Early) movement is partly about investing in financial assets. But you've got to also think about investing in yourself. At the end of the day, that can guarantee a far better return for you.

In this context, trade the minimal amount of time for the money you need to live on, and then spend the rest of your time building your business until it can replace your main income.

At first your time might be spent on figuring out what kind of business to build. As you begin building a business, you might need to do a little more freelancing to finance the business. It may be a slow build. That's fine. It's about putting one foot in front of the other.

Being Efficient

In order to get your "freedom" it's important to find ways to automate your procedures. The better you can trade "one-to-one" to "one-to-many", the more leverage you'll have to build income. The former approach has growth limited to the amount of time available to each client. By writing a book to scale your expertise, for example, the only limit to the number of people you can reach is how many are willing to pay the price of the book.

Many freelancing skills can be scaled in a similar way. It's for you to think about ways to do so. Think about it. If you are a freelancer, you must do everything from high-value client pitches to low-value admin work.

But if you are ready (and only if you're ready) you can leverage your time by hiring help for lower-value tasks. That's why the virtual assistant industry is booming. It can be cheap, particularly if you're using resources from lower-cost locations like the Philippines, and easier than ever before.

Do an inventory on everything you spend your time on and ask if there's someone else than can do this almost as good as me for much cheaper. Look at how much you would price yourself per hour and see whether you can find a cheaper alternative. There will always be tasks that you would prefer to hold onto, whether it's due to privacy or creative reasons. But there are plenty of tasks that can be outsourced, such as preparing expense reports, gathering content for social media posts and doing market research.

The goal is to benefit from multiplying your income without multiplying the time you spend working. Create something that frees you up.

Final Thoughts

Ideally you should target multiple avenues if you are looking to build income online consistently with your specific skillset.

For example, you could have:

1. A website as your "home base" to highlight your skills and blog to show your expertise. This will also allow you to earn money through affiliate marketing and advertising.
2. A presence on social media sites, most notably Facebook and Twitter that will allow you to connect with your "tribe" and redirect people to your website;
3. A presence on a few marketplaces (e.g. Fiverr or PeoplePerHour) or online storefronts (e.g. eBay, Amazon, Bonanza, eCrater or Etsy) to generate income. Relying on a single site is limiting. Admittedly, maintaining a presence in several is a lot of work but the rewards include increased sales.

So, this is the start of your journey.

It's going to be trial and error as a lot of what you first try out may not be what you end up investing your time in.

But as mentioned before, you've got to simply start. If you just stick to "thinking about it", everyone around you will have dipped their toes in and made the money that was meant for you!

Find a mix of side hustles that work for you and be prepared to pick up and drop as you learn the ropes. Good luck!

www.ingramcontent.com/pod-product-compliance
Lightning Source LLC
Chambersburg PA
CBHW021548200526

45163CB00016B/3111